A big wet lick!

"You're too little to help!" said Rob.

"This is a very big hill,"
said the little mouse.

"This is a very big hill
for me to get up,"
puffed the little mouse.

"I am not a hill!"
said the big, sleepy lion.
"I am a lion,
and you are on my back!"

4

"I will eat you for my tea," he said.

"No! Please don't eat me!
A very big lion needs a very big tea, but I am a very little mouse. I'd be a very little tea," said the little mouse.

"Please let me go home!" said the mouse. "I am a very, very little mouse, and not very good to eat."

"If you let me go, I will help you!" said the little mouse.

7

So, the big lion let the little mouse go, and the little mouse ran and ran and ran!

And off went the lion for his tea.

"Help! Help me! Please help me," yelled the lion.
"Help me get out of this trap. The men will come and take me to a zoo!"

"I will not help you.
If I do you will eat me,"
said the rabbit.

11

"I will not help you.
If I do you will eat me,"
said the zebra.

"I will not help you.
If I do you will eat me,"
said the chimp.

"I will.
I will help you,"
said the little mouse.
"I will get you out of the trap."

"Sit still. Just sit very still, and I will get you out of the trap," said the little mouse.

The little mouse bit,

and he bit,

and he bit.

"Thank you little mouse,"
said the lion. "Thank you!"
And he gave the mouse
a big, wet lick!